Library of
Davidson College

With the
compliments
of the
Canada Council

Avec les
hommages
du Conseil des
Arts du Canada

Maple Syrup

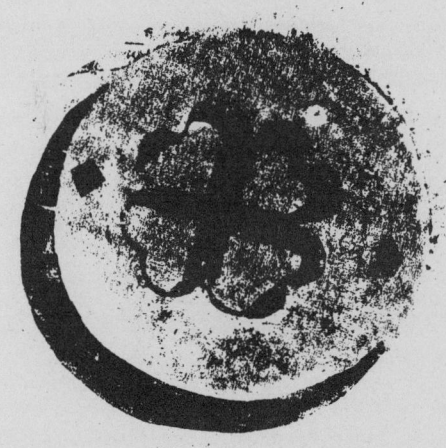

Maple Syrup

by R. D. Lawrence

nelson

664.1
L422m

©R. D. Lawrence 1972
ISBN 0-176-35125-6

77-5295

Contents

1 Foreword

5 How I Learned about Maple Syrup

40 Afterword

58 Recipes

Foreword

How it Began

Perhaps it was a squirrel that taught an Indian that the sap of the maple tree is sweet—a little, chattering red squirrel that climbed up the trunk of a fat, old maple one morning in spring and bit a thin branch.

From the small cut made in the tender bark by the squirrel's razor-sharp teeth the sap flowed, and the squirrel drank, lapping greedily at the cool, sweet juice. Below, a primitive man curiously watched the squirrel at work, wondering why it was drinking the tree sap when there was plenty of clean snow water pooled in hollows all through the maple forest.

When the squirrel was finished the man copied the little animal, making a small cut in the tree with his flint knife and tasting the sap that came from it.

Imagine his surprise when he found that the dripping sap was quite sweet and that when some of it ran down his chin it soon became sticky and stayed sweet! Until that moment he and his tribe had found sweetness only in berries; now here was a tree that cried sugar in fast, crystal-clear tears.

Here was a find! But before he returned with the good news to the tribe, the Indian drank his fill, unconsciously treating his body with the right medicine to drive away the "spring sickness" which, in those times, attacked Indians every year.

This sickness we know now was scurvy. We also know that it makes us ill when our bodies become short of Vitamin C, which is found only in plants, fruits and vegetables. Because the Indians lived almost entirely on meat during the long winters—for they had no way of storing fresh fruit and vegetables during the time of cold—their bodies ran short of Vitamin C, and every spring most of them would become ill with scurvy. To cure themselves they had to wait until the sap in the trees came out of its winter hiding place in the roots; then they would scrape the soft, inner bark off many of the trees, such as poplars and birches, and they would eat this spongy, sap-rich pulp which contained Vitamin C.

Our Indian of long ago probably did not realize at the time that he had found a new cure for the spring sickness. He would learn this later after he had taken the news to the tribe, for the scurvy left his body quickly, and not long after the rest of his tribe had drunk of the sweet sap, they too became cured.

Because he had been curious about the habits of a small squirrel, the Indian did two things. He "invented" maple syrup and he found a quick, good-tasting way to cure scurvy.

Of course, it probably took a little time for the Indians to learn that they had to boil the sap so as to evaporate the water that it contained until all that was left was the sweet, golden syrup. This all happened so long ago that we can only guess today about how it really began. It may be that one of the tribe left in the sun a birch-bark pot in which there was a little sap and after several hours of hot spring sunshine the water was "boiled out" of the sap, leaving a thin but very sweet syrup in the pot.

After that one of the Indians may have heated some stones and put them into a pot of sap, noticing that the red-hot stones boiled out the water much more quickly than the sunshine, in this way getting more and thicker syrup. Then, almost certainly, the Indians reasoned that if they could boil the syrup with hot stones, it would be much faster to set birch-bark "pails" over a fire and evaporate the water that way.

This they did, cleverly fashioning the primitive pails so that the white, easy-to-burn part of the bark was placed on the inside, while the fire-resisting inner bark remained on the outside.

When they had invented this new way of boiling the sap, the Indians began making syrup in large amounts. Each spring they would go into the maple forest with their sap pails, fasten them to trees which they had first cut with their knives so that the sap would flow, and in this manner gather the sweet sap. While some of the tribe looked after the emptying of these pails into bigger, birch bark, gathering pails, others looked after the fires and the boiling of the sap which was brought there in the gathering pails.

This was how the Indians were making maple syrup when the first white men came to North America. There they were, in the forests of Quebec and Ontario in that part of North America which was to become Canada, and in those areas that later were to become the states of Vermont, New York, Pennsylvania, Ohio, Michigan, New Hampshire, Wisconsin, Massachusetts, Maine, Maryland, Minnesota and West Virginia. And these early white men, because of the problems of bringing with them large quantities of sugar from Europe, quickly realized the value of the maple tree.

At first they traded some of their own goods to the Indians in exchange for syrup and maple sugar. Later they began to make their own syrup, at first using the same methods as the Indians, later making large, cast-iron pots for boiling the sap, using metal pails for gathering it, and inventing metal spiles or taps which go into the tree and through which the sap runs out.

So, through a squirrel teaching an Indian, and an Indian teaching a white man, the age of maple syrup was born. The maple tree has become a unique part of Canadian and American history and culture, for maple syrup is made in no other countries in the world.

How I Learned About Maple Syrup

Which is a Maple?

There I was, one morning in February, up to my waist in snow and surrounded by bunches and bunches of bare trees. "Which ones are the maples?" I asked myself as I stood there. And I was so worried about the question that I hardly felt the cold that was nipping at my ears and nose like some sharp-toothed little animal.

You see, I had just bought a 350-acre farm. On eighty of those acres there were thousands of maple trees—or so I had been told—and the trouble was that I didn't know a maple from an elm—not without their leaves on, that is. The trouble, too, was that I had agreed to start making maple syrup that very spring. If I knew little about maple trees, I knew even less about maple sugar or how to make it. That's why I was a bit scared that day.

I knew all kinds of things about pines and birches and balsams and practically all of Canada's trees *except* the maples and the elms. I had spent a lot of time exploring the Canadian wilderness, right up to the Yukon and the Northwest Territories where elms and maples don't grow. But right now it wasn't much good my knowing how to make tea out of the tips of hemlock and spruce, or how to make quite a good salad out of the tender, inner bark of the white poplar. That didn't help at all as I stood and looked at those great big trees that grew around me.

"Mr. Lawrence," I said to myself, for I am always very polite when I speak to me. "You really *must* learn all about the maple."

Since I was really being quite reasonable with myself, not scolding or anything, I listened to my advice, and that very day I sort of went to school to study maples. Well, it really wasn't school, but I did find a teacher, a good one. His name was Ernest Pierce. He was not too tall and quite thin and he was a very old and very wise man. I had bought my farm from him. Of all people, I thought, Mr. Pierce would be able to tell me all that I wanted to know about the trees.

Away I went, not worrying anymore, even ignoring that long, strange building that huddled on the edge of the woods. That was mine, too; it went with the farm and Mr. Pierce had told me it was a sugar house. But I didn't know much about it then.

Ten minutes later I was in the big old farm house that was built more than a hundred years ago. In the kitchen, sitting in a rocking chair, was Mr. Pierce, a knowing look in his eyes and a small smile on his lips.

Seeing him sitting there so quiet and confident, I was glad

he had agreed to stay at the farm until we had finished making syrup. I just *knew* I was going to need him. And I think that *he* knew it too!

"Mr. Pierce," I said and had my mouth open for the next words when he waved a long thin hand towards a chair.

"I know," his voice interrupted me. "You want to learn about the sugar bush."

I sat down. I wasn't really surprised that he had guessed what I wanted; I think my questions were written all over my face.

That was how my maple education started, sitting in a warm farm kitchen drinking tea and just listening as Mr. Pierce talked ....

There are, I learned, ten different kinds of maples in Canada and thirteen in the United States, but only two give sap sweet enough to make syrup. One is the sugar maple, which tree experts call *Acer saccharum,* the other is the black maple, or *Acer nigrum.* Both grow in Canada and the United States.

Only the sugar maple grew on our farm. When I asked why, Mr. Pierce explained that the black maple, which is quite similar to the *Acer saccharum,* only grows in a small, southwestern part of Quebec and in southern Ontario and, of course, in the United States.

Why could one not make maple syrup from the sap of the other maples? I asked Mr. Pierce. He smiled and said that one could, because sugar is found in the sap of all maple trees. In fact, the early settlers did just that when they made syrup for their own use. Then, when more people came to North America and syrup was made for sale, the syrup makers found that there just wasn't enough sugar in the other maples to make the work of tapping them worth while.

Of course, what I really wanted to know that morning was how I could tell the difference between a maple tree and an elm tree, so that when we started to make syrup I wouldn't tap the wrong ones. Mr. Pierce told me, explaining the difference in the bark, in the size of the trees, and even in the way their branches grow.

Sometimes the sugar maple grows 130 feet tall and has a trunk that is five feet around, although as a rule they grow to a height of ninety feet and their trunks measure between two and three feet around. Apart from giving the sap from which the syrup is made, maple wood is valuable for making flooring and furniture and many other things that need a wood that is hard and strong.

Mr. Pierce explained that I would have to make sure that my bush stayed "good and healthy". How could I keep it healthy? Well, he said, if young trees grew too near each other they shot up towards the light and just grew tall and thin, and didn't grow many branches. That sort of tree wouldn't give much sap and it wasn't much good for cutting up as lumber. The maple bush had to be "thinned out" so the trees would have growing room.

"You've also got to cut down the old trees, the ones that don't give much sap anymore," he said.

These big trees, even though they look good, are dangerous because some of their big branches may break off and crash down and kill other, good trees, or maybe even fall on top of people!

I began to learn that day that looking after a maple forest wasn't as easy as I had thought. It was rather like taking care of a garden, but a very big garden! If it wasn't kept neat and tidy, if the "weeds", the poor quality trees, were not taken out, it wouldn't give much maple syrup and even the valuable wood of the trees would spoil.

It was a bit scary. I hadn't thought about all these things when my friend Alvin Adams had suggested that we go into partnership and buy Mr. Pierce's farm. Alvin had told me all about the maples and how we could make money with the syrup and it seemed like a good idea when we were talking about it.

Neither of us had made syrup before, but we thought it would be easy, a bit like milking a cow; you know, you just let the cow eat grass and she comes in twice a day and she gives you her milk. Well, now I know that milking a cow isn't easy either, and so does Alvin. But we learned how to make syrup, eventually, and we had a lot of fun doing it. But we sure needed Mr. Pierce to tell us how!

The Sap Season

It was a month later, time to start preparing the maple bush for gathering the sap which was even then getting ready to climb upwards, out of its wintering place in the roots of the trees. Alvin Adams and Mr. Pierce and I walked through the deep snow to the evaporator house.

The snow was getting soft and it made walking difficult. I wondered if we would ever be able to clear it from the trails that criss-crossed the maple bush. There seemed to be so much of it.

"How do we start?" I asked Mr. Pierce.

"You've got to clear the trails first, so we can drive the tractor and wagon through 'em; else we can't get the equipment out there," he answered.

Alvin, who is a quiet man most of the time, scratched his head, looked at the snow and then turned to me.

"I reckon I'll fetch the loader down."

The loader was his yellow bulldozer which was fitted with a bucket-scoop. It was old, but somehow Alvin always managed to keep it going. Now he would have to load it on his truck and drive the two miles from his place to the farm. He left soon afterwards to get it, while I followed Mr. Pierce into the evaporator house.

The building was sixty feet long by eighteen feet wide and divided into four parts. The roof was built in the shape of a big capital A with a smaller A sitting on top of it. It was really two roofs with a space between them. This space was walled on both sides by metal flaps that could be lowered to let out the steam that fills the evaporator house when the sap is boiling. If the roof was not built in this way, the inside of the building would get so full of steam that no one would be able to see anything.

As Mr. Pierce opened the front door and we went inside, I found myself in a room eighteen feet wide by twelve feet deep. Mr. Pierce began showing me some of the equipment that was in the sugar house and telling me what it was used for. In about five minutes I was quite confused and I couldn't remember what was what.

"Don't worry about it," he said, noticing how puzzled I was. "You'll learn about all this stuff later, when we start boiling."

I wondered if I ever *would* learn, there seemed to be so much to know. But because he was so confident, and, I suppose, because there was nothing else that I could do about it, I tried not to let it worry me. And then he opened another door and led me into the room where the evaporator stands.

At first all I could see were the sap pails, hundreds and hundreds of them, stacked one on top of the other and seeming to fill the whole evaporator room. In fact, there were twenty-four hundred pails in there and they crowded around the back end of the evaporator. Mr. Pierce patted one of the stacks of pails affectionately.

"We've got to hang these," he said quietly, a tiny smile lurking on his lips. I looked at the pails and I looked at him. Did he mean we had to hang every single one of those pails? He did. We were going to have to drill holes in some two thousand trees (the big trees are tapped three or four times) with a hand drill, put a spile or tap into each hole, and hang a pail on every little hook that hung from the taps. It looked like a big job—and it was!

While I was still thinking about all the work that those stacks of pails were going to give, Mr. Pierce pushed past them and introduced me to the evaporator. It was *huge!* There it sat, twenty feet long by six feet wide, a monster fireplace with a monster chimney. The thing was built like a long iron box without a lid. The fire box, lined with special fire-resisting bricks, gaped at me like some very hungry prehistoric creature. It looked like it was getting ready to bite!

I was a bit afraid of it then, but later on I got quite fond of it and christened it Ernie in honor of Mr. Pierce, because it seemed just as gnarled and as enduring as its namesake.

Balanced on top of the fire box, leaning against each other, were the sap and syrup pans which, Mr. Pierce said, formed the top of the evaporator. When it was time to boil the sap, these pans were lowered and fitted into special grooves that ran all around the fire box so that the pans were actually sitting right on top of the fire and no smoke or sparks could escape around them.

The fire in the evaporator was fed by opening a set of double doors, made of heavy cast iron. Hanging on one wall near the fire doors was a set of long iron pokers with big handles which helped push the wood inside the fire.

At the far end of the evaporator room was a big sliding door. Mr. Pierce opened it and I found myself in a lean-to shed. Here was where the firewood was stored. There were great stacks of wood, cut in lengths of six or seven feet, piled so high that they almost reached the sloping roof.

"I see you've got plenty of firewood," I said to Mr. Pierce.

He shook his head.

"No, I think we're going to have to burn the tires too," he answered.

Burn the tires? What tires? I was really puzzled, until I followed Mr. Pierce out of the shed and there, stacked in the snow, were hundreds of old car and truck tires, and even a few enormous road-grader tires.

"I've been using them for years. They sure make good heat." Mr. Pierce paused, tilted his face nearer to me and said slowly and distinctly, "You've got to have a hot fire to make good syrup, you know."

I didn't know, but I was ready to take his word for it. I wasn't too keen on the idea of burning tires, though, what with the smell and all that black smoke polluting the country. But this was Mr. Pierce's show and I knew him well enough by then to realize that once he had made up his mind about something, there was little that could be done to change it for him. And, sure enough, we *did* burn those tires that year, *and* we set the evaporator house on fire! But that story will come later....

Just then my mind was on other things as I followed my guide to the west side of the evaporator house to another shed that leaned against it. Inside this I saw three enormous, rectangular tanks made out of galvanized sheet metal. These, Mr. Pierce told me, were the storage tanks for the sap. They were connected to each other by galvanized iron pipes, and they were also connected by these pipes to the evaporator. When the tanks were full of sap, the boiling would start, and I remember thinking at the time that it was going to take an awful lot of sap to fill those big containers. Actually, two tanks held a thousand gallons of sap and the third 750 gallons, and I suppose that really *is* a lot of sap!

While we were in the storage tank shed we heard the engine of Alvin's truck, so we left and returned to the sugar house where Mr. Pierce stored the spiles and the lids of the sap pails. At the time I didn't know that the sap pails needed to have lids, so I asked why this was so, although if I had thought about it for a bit I probably would have figured it out for myself. You see, the cleaner you keep the sap when you are making syrup, the less work you will have and the better the syrup and taffy will be. The lids are attached to the spiles by means of a straight piece of wire that slides through a place in the lid, making a hinge, so that the lids can be easily lifted when one must empty the sap from the pails. By keeping the lids on, twigs and old leaves don't fall into the pails.

By the time I had been told why the lids were needed, Alvin's bulldozer was creaking and clanking its way towards us, its motor chugging quietly. Behind Alvin and the bulldozer trotted nine-year-old Johnny Adams who had come to help.

Because we had the bulldozer, clearing the snow from the trails was going to be relatively easy, so we let Alvin and his bulldozer go ahead while Johnny, Mr. Pierce and I started getting things ready. First we had to wash the pails and the lids and the spiles, sterilizing them with Javex, for it is important to keep everything really clean. That took quite a while, as you can imagine, what with all those pails *and* all those taps and lids. But at last it was all done and by then Alvin had cleared almost half of the trails. By this time, too, his brother Aut (short for Austin) had arrived to help, so there were five of us to do the work.

The Tapping

When Aut joined us Mr. Pierce said it was time to start tapping; this job should be done *before* the sap starts to run, so that when the weather begins to warm up during the day, all the spiles are in the trees and all the pails are in place, ready to catch the sap as it drips through the taps. Knowing when to tap is really a matter of experience mixed with luck. After many years of syrup making Mr. Pierce knew to within a few days when the sap run could be expected, but, of course, no one can tell for *sure* because it all depends on the weather. That's where the luck comes in. If you're lucky, you get it just right; if not you may tap too early, and have to wait or risk a heavy snowfall on your cleared trails; or you may be too late, which is worse, for you lose quite a bit of sap, which escapes not only up the tree and into the branches, but pours out of the newly-drilled holes before the spiles and pails can be put in.

    I don't mean that it *really* pours out like water out of a tap, but it certainly leaks out. When you make syrup, you need all the sap you can get if you expect to make a profit. It takes, in fact, about *forty gallons* of sap to make *one gallon* of syrup, depending on the amount of sugar that is in the sap.

    I suppose that different syrup producers have slightly different ways of setting out to tap the trees. Some I know still use horses to draw their wagons, whereas we used a tractor, but by and large, if one uses pails for the job instead of the modern plastic tubing, which I shall talk about later, there are only small differences in the way the work is done.

Here is how we did it. Aut Adams went ahead with a hand brace equipped with a special wood-boring bit and started tapping the trees. Following him was the tractor, driven by Mr. Pierce, drawing a flat-bed wagon loaded with pails, lids, spiles and hooks.

Before we set out, while Aut was getting a head start on the tapping, Mr. Pierce told me what to do. The spiles had to be tapped in with a hammer, firmly but not too deep, otherwise the end of the spile, which has a little cross cut into it to allow the sap to flow through it, would hit against the wood of the tree and would become blocked. Also, the spiles could not be tapped in too loosely, or the sap would run out around them instead of through them.

As I finished putting in each spile—to which, of course, the lid was already attached—Johnny would come along and hang a pail on it. In this way we worked all that day, stopping for a short lunch break and returning to the bush for more drilling and tapping-in of spiles and hanging of pails, until, at last, it was too dark to work any more. To be honest, I was glad when the sun set, for I was tired by then and I know the others were too. It is hard work tapping a bush. It's not so much the weight of the things one must carry, but all the walking about in the deep wet snow, going from one tree to another, often stumbling on dead branches that are buried by the snow, while your hands get cold and your feet and pants get both wet and cold, sometimes right up to the knees in the places where the snow has drifted into mounds. But it must be done or there's no syrup at the end of the season.

Next morning we were back at work at eight o'clock, but by then Alvin had finished breaking trail and he and Aut began to drill the tap holes. Now we went faster, so fast, in fact, that Johnny and I were hard-pressed to keep up with the drillers. We were glad of the break at noon and twice as glad when we learned that Alvin's other son, Jim, aged seventeen, was going to help as well.

After lunch I asked Mr. Pierce if I could do some drilling, for I wanted to try it. He agreed, but he first told me how to do the job properly. I already knew how far in I had to drill, but Mr. Pierce insisted on watching as I bored the first holes, making sure I slanted the drill bit upwards just the right amount, so the sap would be able to run down into the spile and so drip in the pail.

He also explained that the new drill holes should be made about six inches away from last year's holes because it takes a tree about 10 years to grow enough new wood to fill the drill holes.

"You've got to drill like a corkscrew," he said to me.

Of course I didn't know what he was talking about, but he was patient and told me that trees must be drilled in a spiral fashion; each year one drills a hole six inches away from the last one and a few inches higher up, so that by the time you reach a place on a tree where you can no longer work comfortably because it is getting too high from the ground, the lowest and oldest tapholes are fully healed and you can start again at a lower level. If a tree is drilled too high up it is difficult to empty the pails when the sap starts running.

After I had drilled about a dozen trees Mr. Pierce seemed satisfied with my work and he returned to driving the tractor, while I went happily on, drilling one tree after another. At first I was pleased with my new job. I still had to tramp through the deep snow; now all I was carrying was a brace and bit instead of a pile of lids and spiles. But after about an hour of hand drilling into green wood my arms and wrists began to ache and even though I was wearing heavy leather mitts, I started getting blisters on my hands. In this way I discovered that the best way to work when tapping a maple bush is to change jobs with your companions every now and then, taking a rest from one job by doing another. And that is what we did. Three days later the tapping was all done.

We had cleared the trails, drilled nearly two thousand trees, tapped in 2,400 spiles and hung the same number of pails. I remember I walked into the middle of our bush, stood at a cross-roads of two trails and looked around me. Wherever I looked stood maple after maple, each carrying one, two, three or four pails. It was a great sight for me and I looked up through the branches at the sky which had been dull all day. There towards the west, for it was already late afternoon, the sun was beginning to show through the clouds. I felt it was a good omen. The way it turned out, it was.

The Sap Run

As I stood there Mr. Pierce came up to talk to me. He too looked at the sky and he said he thought the sap would start running any day. I asked him to tell me about the effect of the weather on the sap.

"Well, I suppose you could say that the best sap weather is when you get a hard frost at night and a good sunny day to follow, melting the frost and making the temperature go up to 40 or 50 degrees," he told me.

Standing in the maple woods I learned that trees that lose their leaves every autumn, such as the maples, must put away reserves of food to carry them through the winter and to give them the extra energy they need to make new leaves in the spring. For this purpose they store their extra "food" in their roots, and it is this food, mixed with water that the roots take from the soil, that forms the sap.

Sap is rather like the blood in our veins and like it, too, it flows through "veins" in the trees, so when the sun begins to get warmer in early spring, the sap starts flowing up the tree in large amounts, preparing to feed the budding leaves. One of the ingredients of the tree's food supplies is sugar and that's where the syrup comes from. If the sap is rich in sugar, it takes less of it to make syrup.

"The amount of sugar in the sap depends on a lot of things, like the kind of soil the trees are growing in, the size and age of the tree and the growing room that a tree has," Mr. Pierce told me.

Trees that grow in the open tend to have more branches, and thus more leaves, and since the leaves "make" the food, such trees have a better supply of sugar unless they are too young or too old.

"Of course, you know," said Mr. Pierce, frowning, "sometimes we get a bad year when the weather isn't right and the sap run is poor. You don't make much money then."

So I found out that maple syrup producers, like all farmers, depend a great deal on the weather. If it is kind, they make lots of syrup; if it is not, they go to a great deal of work—for they don't know what the weather is going to be like before they start tapping—and end up, if they are lucky, just clearing expenses. And that's why maple syrup seems to cost so much; it must pay for all the work of making it and leave a little over to pay for the bad times. But the weather was good to us that year. Two days later the sap started to run.

Sap Gathering

It was a beautiful morning of early Canadian spring. By eight o'clock the sun was actually warm and the snow and frost had already been melting for several hours. In the maple woods the sap was dripping into the pails with that tinkling, musical rhythm that is so good to hear. When I lifted the lid of one of the pails it was already half full, which meant that the run had started during the night.

"Sometimes it does that. In a real good year I've seen it run all night," Mr. Pierce said later, as we were filling the tractor with gasoline in readiness for the sap gathering.

When Alvin and his son Jim arrived—Johnny was at school and Aut had gone to his regular job—we lifted the five-hundred-gallon gathering tank onto the wagon, fastening it down securely. Next we went to the sugar house and collected the big gathering pails with which we were going to empty the tree pails and fill the gathering tank. When we each had one of these Mr. Pierce climbed onto the tractor and headed for the maple bush, the three of us following behind.

Soon Mr. Pierce stopped the tractor on the first trail. We began emptying pails. Carrying the gathering pail in our left hand, we would go to a tree, lift the lid from a pail with our right hand, lean towards the tree and hold the lid up while we tipped the tree pail, pouring the sap into the gathering pail. I found the work tricky at first. Now and then I would splash sap all over myself in my efforts to hold up the lid and tip the tree pail at the same time. My trousers were quickly soaked with sap, and sticky, but I was enjoying myself and the gathering tank was beginning to fill up.

After about an hour of pail tipping and sap gathering, I began to get the hang of it and by the time we had made three trips with the gathering tank and had emptied the first five hundred pails or so, I was good at the job.

The way we did it was really quite simple. The tractor and wagon travelled along the trails, stopping now and then to wait for us as we went from tree to tree to get the sap. Sometimes we would have to empty four or five pails into our gathering pail before this became full; at other times just two sap pails would fill it.

Some trees give more sap than others, depending on their size and age, and when lots of sap dripped from the tree, the two-and-a-half gallon pails would be full to the brim; two of these would fill our five-gallon gathering pails.

After a whole day of carrying the heavy gathering pail through the deep, soft snow, I was exhausted. Full of sap they weighed almost sixty pounds and each time we went to pour them into the gathering tank we had to lift them up to shoulder height. I wasn't used to that sort of work and my arms and shoulders and legs were quite stiff when we shut off the tractor that evening. Yet I was satisfied.

The sap was running well, dripping, dripping, dripping all over the maple bush. We had made five trips with the gathering tank, putting about four hundred gallons of sap into it each trip—we couldn't fill it right up or the sap would spill out of it as the wagon bobbed and dipped along the uneven trails. Now we had about two thousand gallons of sap in the storage tanks and we were going to start boiling that very night, right after supper.

We *had* to work that night. It looked as though the sap was going to keep running all night, and if it did, the pails would be full by morning. If we didn't start that night our storage tanks would become full before we had emptied the next day's run and this would waste sap by overfilling the pails and dripping onto the ground.

Alvin and I had agreed that when the time came to evaporate the sap, I would stay in the evaporator house with Mr. Pierce and learn from him how to do the job, while Alvin and Jim carried on gathering sap. But that night Alvin would come back after his meal and help us get Ernie, the evaporator, started. He was also going to bring with him a couple of extra gasoline lanterns, for there was no electricity in the evaporator house.

Ready to Boil

We were in the evaporator house working by the yellow light of three lanterns. Outside was the darkness and the snow and the trees, the musical notes of sap as it plinked into the pails clearly audible in the night. Above the roof of the evaporator house the green-blue stars sparkled brightly. It was a beautiful night in early spring, moonless, but somehow perfect for the job we were about to start.

Alvin was getting ready to light a fire inside of Ernie. Mr. Pierce and I were lowering the sap and syrup pans, fitting them into their special grooves so that they sat flush on top of the fire box, sealing it with their blackened bottoms.

Our evaporator held three huge sap pans and three smaller syrup pans. The sap pans were six feet by six feet square, and when sitting on Ernie, one in front of the other, they were connected by syphons. The bottoms of these pans are crimped, or corrugated, to increase the heat surface and so help to evaporate the water more quickly.

Hooked onto one corner of the first sap pan was the sap control box and inside of this was the sap control float. This box and its float, made of sheet metal, work exactly like the tank of a modern flush toilet. They allow the sap that is piped in from the storage tanks to run into the pans. When the pans are filled to the proper level, the float rises in the control box and shuts off the flow; when the level in the pans has dropped because of evaporation, the float drops also and the sap starts flowing again. In this way the sap is fed into the pans automatically.

As I helped Mr. Pierce prepare the evaporator, I learned about each step in the operation, discovering that evaporators are built so that they slope gently towards the syrup pans. This helps the syphons to pass the sap from pan to pan.

By the time that Mr. Pierce and I had fitted the six pans in place on top of the evaporator and connected them all by their syphons, Alvin had set the fire. All that was needed now was to let in the sap, fill the pans and put a match to the kindling.

"You must put sap in the pans before you light the fire, you know," Mr. Pierce spoke as he was turning the valves that control the flow of sap from the storage tanks.

"Yes, I remember you explained that the other day. The pans would burn if the fire was started first, wouldn't they?" I replied, pleased at the chance to let him know that I was learning a little about this job.

He nodded and went on turning the valves and the sap began gushing into the pans, gurgling and frothing as though it was full of detergent. While the pans were filling we sat and chatted about syrup making, Alvin and I asking questions and Mr. Pierce answering them.

In this way I discovered that what went on in the

evaporator wasn't as mysterious as I had thought. The sap is kept at a constant boiling temperature and the water is evaporated from it in the form of steam. As it loses water the sap begins to thicken. Because the evaporator is built on a slope towards the syrup pans, and because these hold less liquid than the big sap pans, the level in the syrup pans is lowered first by the evaporation.

Now the syphons begin to work, for as soon as the level in these pans drops, each syphon sucks in more liquid from the pan behind, in this fashion keeping a constant flow of gradually thickening sap moving from the sap pans to the syrup pans.

After several hours of boiling, the liquid in the syrup pans is thick and heavy; it has lost so much water that it is turning into syrup. At this point the syphon that connects the last sap pan to the first syrup pan is shut off. Now the pans are divided into two groups. There are the big deep sap pans which hold quite a watery sap, and the smaller, shallower syrup pans that hold a thick golden liquid that is not quite syrup.

If the syphon that connects the last sap pan to the first syrup pan is not shut off, the thinner sap would mix with the heavier sap, preventing proper evaporation of the syrup. This, when it is finished, must have 65.5 per cent sugar content when tested with a Brix hydrometer, and must weigh thirteen pounds and two ounces to the gallon.

When the syphon that connects the syrup pans to the sap pans is shut off, care must be taken with the fire. If it burns too fiercely, the syrup will burn or boil over; if it does not give out enough heat, the finishing of the syrup will take too long; if it takes too long, one does not draw off enough syrup every day. It is very important to make the right amount of syrup *every day*, otherwise the syrup producer loses money; the evaporator must work to maximum capacity at all times if one is going to make the right amount of profit. In other words, if one takes too long to make syrup, labour costs go up and this means that the cost per gallon of syrup goes up also.

By the time that Mr. Pierce had finished explaining all of this to us, the pans were full to the right levels and Alvin put a match to the fire. At once a great roar filled the evaporator room as the wood and paper caught fire and the flames were sucked towards the great chimney. I went outside to look at the smoke as it puffed up into the sky. It was quite a sight: a thick white column of smoke shot straight up into the air, then started spreading like a mushroom and drifted upwards, blown towards the east by a slight west wind. Even outside I could hear the fire roar. Suddenly the white smoke turned to black. I knew right away what had happened. They had fed Ernie a tire! I went inside. Sure enough, Alvin and Mr. Pierce were just closing the furnace doors and now Ernie was really roaring, just as though he was angry, or had indigestion from the tire.

The steam started to rise from the pans. It came slowly at first, but within minutes more and more steam filled the sap house and at last we had to lower the metal flaps above because we just couldn't see each other anymore. The evaporator house reminded me of a steam bath built inside the heart of a volcano. And then I noticed the smell. It was faint at first, then grew stronger. It was the smell of maple syrup.

Presently Mr. Pierce came up and gave me a skimmer, a thing that looked like a small hand shovel which was full of small holes. He told me to skim the froth off the sap pans with it. I went to these pans and looked into them through the steam and saw at once what I had to do. Inside the pans thick froth had formed; I started scooping it off, slopping it into an old sap pail.

It looked a bit like the froth that comes when one boils a pot full of potatoes and Mr. Pierce said that it was formed by small bits of solid impurities that were in the sap.

"You get sugar sand in the sap, you know. And even in the syrup," he told me.

What is sugar sand? Well, it is a sort of very fine sand that is sucked out of the ground by the roots of the trees and carried up with the sap. This sand contains many of the minerals that trees need in order to make their food. But we didn't want it in our syrup. So some of it was skimmed off the sap pans, the rest was filtered out of the syrup when this was drawn off, and the last bits that might have gone through the filters were allowed to sink down to the bottom of the settling tanks when the syrup was poured into them. Now I knew why they were called settling tanks.

At about eleven o'clock that morning Mr. Pierce produced a hydrometer, scooped some syrup out of the last syrup pan, poured it into a little metal pot and put the hydrometer into it. It tested 64 per cent.

"It's getting close," he said, pouring the syrup back into the pan and washing the hydrometer pot and the hydrometer in boiling sap.

Then, to my surprise, he asked Alvin to put another tire into Ernie. Alvin looked a little startled too, and obviously thought that with the syrup so close to being ready, we should not increase the heat too much. But he did as he was told and poked a truck tire deep into Ernie's insides. A moment later the evaporator roared and rumbled again, and the chimney, which wasn't too new, began to get red hot. Alvin and I looked at each other; we were worried. Mr. Pierce didn't seem to mind.

Suddenly the syrup started boiling, rising quickly in the pan and threatening to boil over the sides. Mr. Pierce worried this time. He hurried and got some cold sap and poured a little into the syrup pans. The syrup settled down. Then Mr. Pierce announced quite firmly that he was going for a walk! He left.

Alvin and I stood by the syrup pans, watching them, for they were again threatening to boil over. Just as they began to bubble a little wildly again I poured more cold sap into them.

"They sometimes use cream for that," Alvin said. I remembered that I had read somewhere that in the old days, maple syrup makers used to hang a piece of pork fat over the top of the syrup pot, so that if it started to boil, rising in the pot, it would touch the pork and some of its fat would settle over the syrup; this stopped it from boiling over, because fat is heavier and keeps the syrup down. Cream, which also contains fat, would have a similar effect, while cold sap just simply cooled the syrup and took it off the boil.

"The best thing is not to let it boil over," Alvin said. I agreed, and that very day I determined not to let this happen again. Then I smelt burning wood. It didn't come from Ernie, I knew, because no smoke was getting out of the evaporator.

I remembered the chimney and I looked up. Sure enough, the rafters were scorching. The intense heat made by the truck tire had got the chimney so hot that it had set fire to the roof. All we had to put out the fire was cold sap, which we got from the hose that fed the float box. Scrambling up on one of the beams that supported the walls of the evaporator house, I threw a pail of sap at the roof.

The roof hissed and crackled and great clouds of steam came down. Alvin passed me another pail of sap and I threw this also. Four pails later the rafters were out, Ernie had settled down to a contented crackling, the syrup just nicely steamed and Mr. Pierce came back from his walk.

Just as though nothing had happened he tested the syrup again. It was ready. He smiled as he washed out the hydrometer.

"You need lots of heat to make good syrup, you know," he said, repeating what he had told me earlier.

"Well," I thought, "this should be *great* syrup. We sure did have lots of heat that time!"

As it turned out, it *was* great syrup. Nice and light in colour and just full of maple flavour. I had never tasted anything better than newly-finished syrup, still piping hot out of the syrup pan!

Mr. Pierce had got out the thick felt filters and had fixed one of them onto a stand. Under the stand he put a big clean pail. With a twinkle in his eye he opened the spout that was attached to the syrup pan and a thick, golden flow of syrup spurted out and into the filter. At first it formed small golden beads on the outside of the felt; then, slowly, it began to flow into the pail with a musical note.

After about three gallons of syrup had been filtered into the first pail, Mr. Pierce stopped the flow, put a clean filter and a new pail under the spout and turned it on. Now he tested the syrup again. It had thickened a little and showed 66 per cent on the hydrometer. The level in the syrup pans had dropped and I could see the syphons sucking syrup from the first syrup pan into the second and on into the third, the one we were getting the syrup from. I could actually see the current in the pans as the thinner syrup from the front pans flowed along towards the last pan.

Mr. Pierce next turned to the syphon that connects the sap pans to the syrup pans and got this going again, letting fresh, partly-evaporated sap enter into the first syrup pan. Then he tested the syrup in the last pan once more. It showed 65.5 per cent. Mr. Pierce let the syrup continue to fall into the filter. But he kept testing the sugar content with the hydrometer. Presently the hydrometer showed only 64 per cent and Mr. Pierce cut off the flow.

"That's the first run," he said, turning to me. "The whole batch will test 65.5 or a little better, you know."

He meant that although the last quart or so to come out of the pan only tested 64, the difference was made up because earlier the syrup had been thicker, testing 66 per cent.

This was my first maple syrup. That morning we had made about eight gallons and we were to draw off another two batches of syrup before we shut down the evaporator for the night, making a total, for our first day, of twenty-four gallons. This wasn't bad, considering that Ernie was old and not as efficient as the modern evaporators that are being made nowadays.

That day in the sugar house, I filled the new cans with our

hot maple syrup from the tap fixed to the settling tanks. When I had finished, about an inch of very dark syrup remained in the bottom of the settling tanks. This we would not can, because it contained the last of the sugar sand. Instead we cleaned it all out and put it back in the sap pans, so as not to waste any sugar, for, from there, it would go through again and become skimmed and filtered and settled in the settling tanks.

That first season we made 218 gallons of syrup during the three weeks that the sap ran. When the taps dried up and the buds started opening on the trees, came the work of taking down all the pails, pulling out all the spiles and putting everything away, clean, for next year's sap run. There was almost as much work involved in cleaning all our equipment as there had been in getting it all ready. But it was worth it.

Taffy and Sugar

I have never made taffy or maple sugar, but I learned how from Mr. Pierce. When the syrup is drawn from the evaporator pan it is poured into the settling tanks, and later poured into a pan on top of a *finishing stove,* which looks rather like a small evaporator.

There it is boiled again, evaporating still more water

from it until it becomes extra thick. Depending on what one wants to make—soft ball taffy, hard ball taffy, or maple sugar—the syrup is allowed to thicken, taking it off the heat when it tests 22°F. above the boiling point of water for soft ball or 40°F. above the boiling point for hard ball, or letting it stay in the pan until it has been transformed into sugar, when almost all the water has been evaporated from it. Taffy and sugar are poured into different kinds of moulds when it is hot and then allowed to cool and harden. After that, why, you just eat it!

Plastic Tubing

I made syrup in the old traditional way, but modern maple syrup producers changed their methods about ten years ago. Now many of them have discarded the pails, lids, spiles and gathering tanks. Instead they use plastic tubing, which, after the trees are tapped, is connected from tree to tree and through which the sap runs automatically into the storage tanks.

The trees are still drilled in the same manner, but instead of using spiles, spouts are put into the tap holes. To these spouts the tubing is connected.

Plastic tubing gathers the sap more efficiently and with less work, but not all maple bushes are suitable for this kind of operation. Sometimes the trees are too far from each other and it would take too much tubing to hook them all together. Sometimes, too, a syrup producer does not have enough money to convert his bush from pails to tubing. But most big producers use tubing nowadays.

Tubing Versus Pails

There are advantages and disadvantages to both the pail system for gathering sap and the tubing system. When using pails, these have got to be kept very clean and are difficult to scrub, but more important, the fixing in place of pails, lids and spiles, the emptying of the pails, the carrying of the sap in the gathering tank to the evaporator house, mean a great deal of work and the maple syrup producer must pay more money in wages.

The tubing takes away a great deal of the work, but it *does* have some problems. In the first place, today's squirrels, like their ancestor who showed the Indian how to tap a tree, still like to drink the sweet sap and they often bite right through the plastic tubing in order to get a good long drink. When this happens, the leak must be found, that part of the tubing cut out and a new piece put into its place by using unions, which are short lengths of heavy plastic tube that are just smaller than the tubing and will slip into it at both ends.

Sometimes squirrels do a great deal of damage to the

tubing, so much so, in fact, that some syrup makers are painting a mixture of cayenne pepper and varnish on the tubing, within one foot of the tree, the idea being that when a squirrel starts nibbling on the tubing he gets a mouthful of very hot pepper and decides to leave it alone and get his drink from a tree branch instead.

Sometimes an airlock will form in the tubing, and then the sap will not flow until the air has been removed from the lines. But because the tubing system offers so many labour-saving advantages over the pail system, despite the problems mentioned, it seems certain that all maple syrup producers will, in time, switch to the tubing. But it may take a little time, for producers who are operating in the old way must discard their gathering equipment and spend quite a bit of money to buy tubing and all the other things that must go with it. Even though this will pay off in savings in the future, many small operators just do not have the capital needed to make the change.

Another new development in the syrup industry is the disinfectant tablet which is put into the tap hole after each tree has been drilled. This tablet contains paraformaldehyde, and it prevents the growth of molds (fungus) in the tap hole, and kills other bacteria that might cause the tap-hole to dry up. By preventing bacteria and mold from forming in the drill hole and thus blocking the spile or spout, the sap runs for a longer time and is always clean and fresh.

Back to the Sugar Bush

Now, as I finish this book on maple syrup, the snow is deep in my sugar bush. The deer are taking shelter and the birds of winter, the bluejays and nuthatches and chickadees, are seeking food. It is peaceful and quiet and cold and really quite beautiful in my sugar bush. But before long it will be time to break trail again, to push back the snow and then get ready for another syrup season. And who knows, perhaps this year I shall try the plastic tubing, for I am planning to retire Ernie and to install a smaller, modern evaporator in the old sugar house.

Yet I shall miss big old Ernie. He is part of another time and reminds me of the days when the pioneers were blazing the way for me, using horses and sleighs and having exciting sugaring-off parties, when the children used to pour hot taffy on the snow and eat it, pulling it like a string and letting it down into their mouths like they were eating spaghetti.

All these things have happened in my sugar bush during the last hundred years or so. Some of the trees that are standing there today could tell great stories—if they could talk, that is.

Perhaps one day I shall sit down and tell those stories for them.

Library of
Davidson College

Afterword

Now that you know all about maple-syrup making, perhaps you will want to see for yourself. You don't need to buy a maple bush as I did. Many people go on a day's outing to a nearby bush or join in a town's maple syrup festival.

Let's go!

The trees are tapped...
...the old way...

...or the new way.

The sap is gathered into larger pails...
...then into gathering tanks...

...that are drawn by tractor or horse...
...and taken back to the sugar house.

There the sap goes through the evaporation process...
   ...carefully watched and tested...

...while the impatient onlookers wait for a taste. A few lucky ones lunch on baked beans flavoured with maple syrup.

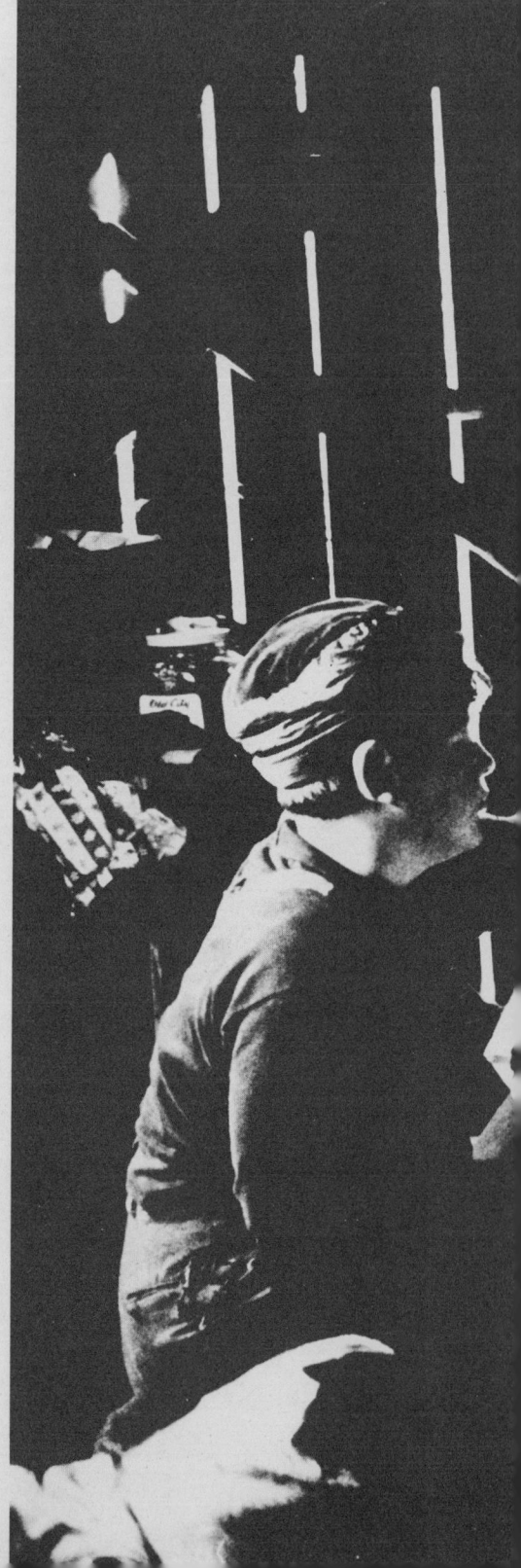

*Finally the syrup is ready
to be poured on snow...
...where it quickly hardens...*

...into a delicious maple taffy!

Recipes

MAPLE TARTS

4 tbsp. butter
4 tbsp. cornstarch (or 6 tbsp. flour)
1 ½ cups maple syrup
½ cup hot water
baked tart shells

Melt butter and blend in cornstarch or flour over low heat. Remove from heat and stir in maple syrup and hot water. Bring mixture to a boil, stirring constantly until mixture thickens. Then continue cooking for 5 minutes, stirring occasionally. Remove from heat and let cool at least 15 minutes. Then spoon into tart shells. Serve plain or garnished with whipped cream or nuts. This makes 24 small tarts.

1 quart parboiled beans
1 cup maple syrup
¼ cup chili sauce
1 tsp. salt
⅛ tsp. pepper
¼ tsp. dry mustard
¼ lb. salt pork
1 small onion, diced

MAPLE BAKED BEANS

Place half of the partially cooked beans in a bean pot or heavy oven dish. Score salt pork and lay on beans; cover with remaining beans. Combine ½ cup maple syrup with remaining ingredients and pour over beans. Add boiling water to cover. Cover dish and bake at 300° for 4 hours. Remove cover, add remainder of maple syrup, and bake for an added half hour or hour, adding water as required.

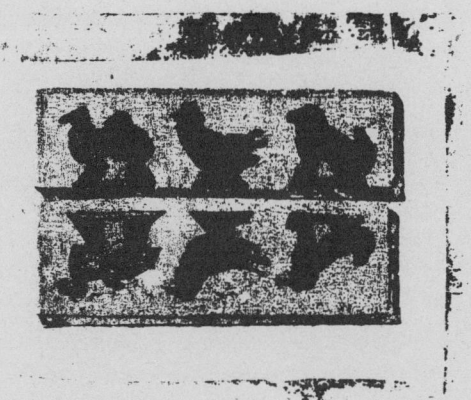

1 cup maple syrup
8 slices bread (¼" to ½" thick)
3 tbsp. butter
3 eggs, beaten
1½ cups milk
few grains salt

MAPLE BREAD PUDDING

Boil syrup 5 minutes. Butter one side of each slice of bread. Dip whole slices in syrup and arrange 2 slices, buttered side up, in bottom of buttered loaf pan. Place remaining slices on top in layers. Make a custard mixture by combining the eggs, any remaining syrup, the salt and milk. Pour over top of bread. Bake in a moderately slow oven (325°) until custard is set and top is golden brown, about 50 minutes. This makes 6 to 8 servings.

1 28-oz. can or 3 cups of strained pumpkin

2 cups maple syrup

½ tsp. each ground ginger, cinnamon and nutmeg

1 tsp. salt

3 eggs

3 cups milk

MAPLE PUMPKIN PIE

Combine pumpkin, syrup, salt and spices. Add well-beaten eggs and milk. Pour into uncooked shells. Bake 40 minutes at 375°. This makes 3 medium-sized pies.

1 cup maple syrup
2 egg yolks, well beaten
½ cup milk
2 egg whites
½ pint (1 ¼ cups) whipping cream

MAPLE ICE CREAM

Measure maple syrup into a large saucepan, bring to a boil and boil vigorously for 5 minutes. Meanwhile combine egg yolks and milk. Slowly add hot syrup, beating constantly until well blended. Chill thoroughly. Beat egg whites until stiff but not dry, then fold into egg mixture. Beat cream until stiff, then fold into mixture. Turn into freezing tray and freeze to a mush. Remove from freezer, stir well and whip with a fork. Return to freezer, stir again after ½ hour, then freeze until firm, 3 to 4 hours. This makes 6 to 8 servings.

MAPLE APPLE PIE

Place sliced apples in 9" pastry-lined pie plate. Mix together melted butter, maple syrup, salt and beaten egg. Pour this mixture over apples. Bake 10 minutes at 425°. Reduce heat to 350° and bake for 25 minutes. Serve hot or cold with whipped cream or ice cream.

½ cup melted butter
¼ tsp. salt
3 sliced apples
1 egg, beaten
1 cup maple syrup
pastry

1 cup maple syrup
½ cup sugar
¼ cup water
1 tbsp. butter
⅛ tsp. cream of tartar

MAPLE PULL TAFFY

Combine all ingredients in a saucepan and boil to 260° or until syrup forms a hard ball when dropped into cold water (not ice water). Immediately pour onto a lightly-buttered platter or tray. As it cools, fold edges to centre being careful not to mix taffy. This is done to prevent the outer part from becoming too hard, and to keep the whole mass at an even temperature and consistency. Allow taffy to cool until a dent is left in it when pressed with the finger, and until it is cool enough to handle. Butter fingers lightly, gather taffy into a ball and pull taffy until it becomes very light-coloured. Stretch and twist into a rope, then cut into 1-inch pieces with scissors. Wrap each piece in waxed paper. This candy retains a taffy-like texture and consistency for about 24 hours. If stored for a longer period, it will soften and have the texture and consistency of a soft mint.

4 cups milk
¼ cup brown sugar
¼ cup maple syrup
¼ tsp. salt
3 tsp. cornstarch
3 eggs, separated
½ tsp. vanilla
1/3 cup nutmeats

MAPLE NUT PUDDING

Heat milk in double boiler. Combine salt, sugar and cornstarch. Blend into maple syrup. Add to scalded milk, stirring constantly until thick. Cook slowly 5 to 10 minutes, stirring occasionally. Beat yolks well; combine with thickened mixture, return to double boiler and cook for two minutes. Remove from heat, add vanilla, and fold in stiffly beaten egg whites.

1 ½ cups milk
1 tbsp. gelatin
¼ cup cold water
2 eggs, well beaten
¾ cup maple syrup
½ tsp. vanilla
¼ cup whipping cream
1 dozen lady fingers

MAPLE ICEBOX CAKE

Heat milk in top of double boiler. Soak gelatin in cold water for 5 minutes. Stir a little of the hot milk into the beaten eggs, then combine with the remaining hot milk in double boiler. Cook, stirring gently until mixture thickens slightly, about 5 minutes. Remove from heat and add soaked gelatin, maple syrup and vanilla, stirring to dissolve gelatin. Chill until mixture is partially set, about 1½ hours. Meanwhile whip cream until stiff. Whip maple mixture until smooth. Fold whipped cream into maple mixture. Pour cream mixture into a plain mold to a depth of about ½ inch. Cut lady fingers in half crosswise. Stand halved lady fingers close together around sides of mold, rounded ends down. Fill mold with remaining cream mixture. Trim ends of lady fingers to surface of cream mixture. Chill until set, about 3 to 4 hours. Unmold for serving. This makes 4 to 5 servings.

1 ham for baking

1 cup maple syrup for each 5 lb. of ham (dark syrup preferred)

MAPLE-BAKED HAM

Bake ham according to your usual method until half done. Remove half the drippings from the pan and reserve for making gravy. Add maple syrup to pan and continue baking with ham covered until done; remove cover a few minutes to brown if desired. Or bake uncovered and baste the ham with the maple syrup from time to time.

MAPLE MOUSSE

18 oz. of maple syrup
8 egg yolks
½ cup cold water
2 envelopes unflavoured gelatin
30 oz. heavy cream, whipped
6 egg whites, lightly beaten

Simmer maple syrup for a few minutes in a large saucepan. Mix egg yolks with 2 tbsp. water and stir in. Dissolve gelatin in remaining water; add, stirring well. Remove from heat and set saucepan in cold water to cool. Continue mixing. Fold in whipped cream to cooled mixture. Add egg whites and mix. Chill overnight. To serve, top with whipped cream, red and green cherries, and pecans.

¾ cup whipping cream
¼ cup maple syrup

MAPLE WHIPPED CREAM

Measure whipping cream into a bowl and chill. Thoroughly chill maple syrup. Beat cream until it begins to thicken. Add maple syrup very gradually, beating constantly, then continue beating until stiff. Serve with angel cake, white cake, or as a filling for cup cakes. It makes about 2 cups.

2 cups maple syrup

½ cup broken nutmeats (pecan or walnut)

PRALINES

Cook syrup until it forms a soft ball in cold water (240°F). Remove immediately from heat and let stand about 1 minute. Pour syrup into lightly-buttered shallow dish. Sprinkle nuts over top. Serve cold by spoonfuls.

2/3 cup uncooked rice
2 eggs, slightly beaten
2/3 cup maple syrup
1 ½ cups milk
few grains nutmeg
¼ tsp. salt
½ cup seedless raisins

MAPLE RICE DELIGHT

Cook rice in boiling salted water. Drain thoroughly. Combine beaten eggs and maple syrup, blending well. Stir in milk to nutmeg, salt, rice and raisins. Turn into buttered oven dish. Oven poach at 350° until set, 1 hour to 70 minutes.

Acknowledgements

Appreciation is expressed to
Mr. W. A. Humphreys, Maple Syrup Extension Specialist,
Ontario Department of Agriculture
and Food, Elmvale, for his helpful advice.

The jacket print is from a lithograph by
Currier & Ives, 1876, courtesy The Travelers Insurance Companies.

Credits for the photographs used in the Afterword
section are as follows:
  1—Information Canada Photothèque, photo by P. Gaudard
  2—Miller Services Ltd., photo by Malak
  3—Information Canada Photothèque, photo by Malak
  4—Information Canada Photothèque, photo by Chris Lund
  5—Photo Forum
  6—Miller Services Ltd., photo by Malak
  7—Miller Services Ltd., photo by Malak
  8—Information Canada Photothèque, photo by Marcel Cognac
  9—Information Canada Photothèque, photo by Marcel Cognac
10—Information Canada Photothèque, photo by Gar Lunney
11—Information Canada Photothèque, photo by Dominion Wide
12—Information Canada Photothèque, photo by J. White
13—Information Canada Photothèque, photo by P. Gaudard
14—Information Canada Photothèque, photo by Malak
15—Miller Services Ltd., photo by Malak
16—Miller Services Ltd., photo by Malak

Recipes are courtesy of the Canada Department of
Agriculture, Ottawa, and the Ontario Department
of Agriculture and Food, Toronto.

Design and illustrations are by Michael van Elsen.

This book has been set in fourteen-point Palatino by Computype.

The paper is eighty-pound Plainfield Offset, Plain Finish.

Printing and binding have been done by The Hunter Rose Company.